COVER PHOTO BY WILLARD CLAY

Publisher: Roy Reiman
Editor: Jean Van Dyke
Publications Editor: Bob Ottum
Art Director: Jim Sibilski
Production: Sally Manich

Printed in U.S.A.
International Standard Book Number:
0-89821-090-9
Library of Congress Catalog Card Number:
89-61836

Sit back...relax...and enjoy
A Year in the Country

WELCOME TO life in the slow lane...a trip down
shaded paths and meandering backroads.

   This second edition of *A Year in the Country*
takes you out of the hectic pace of day-to-day life.
The vivid color photographs, expressive poetry
and eloquent essays in this collection help you
draw a deep breath, slow down and take refuge in
the simple pleasures of life in rural America.

   In these pages, you'll explore the delicate details
and vast vistas that make up country scenery...
from scenic Vermont villages to
placid Michigan lakes...to
rolling Washington
wheat fields. As

you page through *A Year in the Country*, you'll
watch flames crackle in a wood stove...enjoy the
first golden glimpse of daffodils...snuggle under a
hand-made cotton quilt as you listen to the summer rain on the roof of an old farmhouse and walk
through the amber glories of an autumn woods.

   Give yourself a respite from everyday cares.
Share the wit, warmth, comfort and charms of coun-
try life...meet the people and visit the places
that make country so very special.
So, relax...sit back and savor
A Year in the Country.

A Year in the ❖ COUNTRY

26

40

Shhhh...Listen—Spring's Overture Begins

YOU hear it before you see it. The first notes sound...the drip, drip, drip of melting snow, mimicking a drummer tapping the rim with his sticks, held back by the Great Director with a quieting finger over His lips.

The symphony builds. A woodwind sighs a last cold breath through still-bare branches. A late, wet snow mutes early buds impatient to sing spring's song.

The pace picks up. The rhythmic drop becomes a noisy patter, joined by a brassy rush as streams are freed from icy coats.

Finally there's the loud cymbal *crash* of lake ice breaking, and a waterfall trumpets down a mountain! The curtain is up.

These photos record this prelude of nature's winter-to-spring transition...one that crescendoes into a glorious bravura performance. Look. *Listen.* Enjoy!

SHIMMERING SHEEN of Vernal Falls cascades over a giant step formed by glaciers, and spray from the 317-ft. waterfalls frosts the surrounding trees and rocks in scenic Yosemite National Park.

FROSTED FRAMEWORK of lacy trees surrounds serene So. Dakota log barn.

SUNLIGHT SPARKLES diamond-like through spears of asymmetric icicles.

Tom Algire

8

FourbyFive

West Light/Jim Brandenbe

Piotr Kapa

SUSPENDED ANIMATION results from ripples frozen in concentric convolutions in this placid North Carolina stream.

SNOWBOUND SPIKES of yucca knife upward through subsiding end-of-season snowbank in northwest Utah.

Ron Goulet

SUNSHINE'S WARMTH encourages crocuses (left) determined to push through the snowcover in Maine. Top photo, a March ice storm covers an Iowa farm with a transparent glaze. Above, ice drips into transparent stalactites, giving barbed wire a surreal look.

Gabe Palmer/The Stock Market

BREAKUP BEGINS as ice moves out on Hudson River in New York State, piling slab on slab in random heaps, mounds.

STUBBORN PATCHES of snow cling tightly to rocks and marsh grass along the banks of the Merced River in California's Yosemite National Park, as winter begins losing its grip and spring marches in.

MELTING SNOW dimples around grass in sun-striped Texas scene, below left.

FROSTED TREES take on an aura of a master painting in scene below captured by an alert Minnesota cameraman.

DAFFODILS IN DELUGE are fore-taste of springtime sights, as late winter snow gives way to early spring rains. Gritty flowers flourish in the moist environment, and crane their necks toward seldom-seen sun.

BURGEONING BLOSSOMS fill the senses, starting with Christmas rose above left). Earlycomers in western Wisconsin, marsh marigolds and the inelegantly named skunk cabbage add first touch of green. And wildflowers on grand scale carpet California hills, left.

OUTBURSTS OF YUCCA punctuate dunes in White Sands National Monument in New Mexico. And when you turn the page, you'll see spring's official arrival in a colorful display of wildflowers splashing brightness across the landscape in Colorado's Rockies.

I SLIP quietly from under the pile of quilts at 5:30 on a cold winter morning, and wrap a robe around myself. It's chilly in the hallway as I pad, slipper-footed, to the kitchen.

The kitchen is still warm. Our trusty wood stove, the workhorse of our heating system, has held its fire all night. I stir its hot embers back to life, make an adjustment to the damper and add two logs. The stove will soon have the kitchen end of the house toasty.

It takes a little longer in the living room. The ashes in the fireplace are cold—last night's cozy blaze long dead. I rip a sheet of newspaper, crumple the pieces and set them in the center of the fireplace.

I stack thin cedar strips Lincoln-log fashion over the newspaper, open the damper and turn off the lamp before striking a match. I like to watch the fire blossom in the darkness—I've seen it happen a thousand times, but still it's a magical moment.

I know it would be more efficient if we installed an insert in our fireplace, and someday we'll probably do it. We'd get more heat from less wood. But we'd give up something, too, something that's hard to define.

If you've ever sat before an open fire and stared mesmerized into the flames, you know what I'm talking about. Firelight stirs something deep within you, some memory that reaches back before your birth to the days when the only shelter a man had was the ring of light cast by his campfire.

Even here, surrounded by the sturdy walls of my modern home, I feel it. I take great pride in laying up a neat fire. I feel enormous satisfaction as the flames lick up the stack of cedar sticks and catch hold of the small logs across the top.

My husband tells me I'm wonderful to get up early in the morning to get the house warm before waking him and our daughter. I'm certainly not going to contradict him, but the truth is that it's no sacrifice on my part. I love to do it. I am the fire maker, the guardian of the hearth. In the flickering light of my fire, I feel a kinship with the early settlers of this land, with the Indians who were here before them, and with the most ancient an-

Firelight Dreams

By Judy Sizemore of McKee, Kentucky

cestors of mankind who first learned to make light in the darkness and warmth in the cold.

I return to the kitchen and put a pot of water on the stove, then slip out the back door to check the sky.

Yesterday the stars were blotted out by thick layers of cold, gray clouds. All day long the sun refused to shine, and the clouds seemed to press down on me, damp and miserable. Sometime during the night a front must have passed through, sweeping the clouds away, for this morning is crystal clear. The stars glitter in a far-flung sky, like diamonds thrown across black velvet. It will be clear today but bitter cold.

My dog comes up behind me and presses his cold nose against my hand. I reach down to scratch his ears in a gesture that is so familiar it has become a sort of ritual between us. He follows me back into the house. I stop in the kitchen to make a cup of lemon balm tea and a slice of toast with strawberry jam. By the time I get back to the living room, he is already lying before the hearth, paws outstretched to the warmth.

I throw a couple of larger logs on the fire, then sit back in the rocker, sipping my tea, watching the flames, and dreaming in the firelight. In a way these winter mornings are a climax of our country year. In the spring I picked the strawberries and made the jam. In late summer I gathered and dried the lemon balm, and all summer and fall we cut and split and stacked the precious wood so that now I sit in an island of luxury, my thoughts flowing as smoothly as water in a well-worn creek bed.

Spring, summer and fall are the active months, the outdoors months when the big jobs get done. Crops are grown and harvested, fences are put up, barns are built.

Winter is different. It's a time for creativity, for knitting, quilting, writing, painting and dreaming, for talking and planning and dreaming again.

I suppose some people prefer to live in the city in a house where the temperature is automatically regulated all year round and the differences between the seasons are as small as possible. For me, I'll take the country life and the cold mornings warmed by an open fire.

Silver Moire

Sleek winding lengths of watered silk
draw ribbons through the hills
Where waterfalls of crystal spray
spill effervescent frills.

The rippling silver streaks flow free
with trim of lacy froth
To tie rich gifts of meadow gems
in yards of jade green cloth.

—*Marianne McFarland McNeil of Amarillo, Texas*

There's More Than One Way to Build a Barn!

TO SOME PEOPLE, barns are barns. But to a knowledgeable observer of the countryside, to say that one barn is like another is akin to likening lightning and lightning bugs.

The scenes here offer photo evidence that barns come in as many varieties as flowers and trees. Noticing these differences will give you a great-

Jerry Irwin

Kenneth C. Poertner

er appreciation for the country the next time you take a backroads route.

Each barn stands as a silent sentinel of the hopes, dreams, hard work and cooperation of its builders.

The barn was often the first building raised on newly settled land... and often it was built better than the house. After all, sheltering livestock, grain, hay and equipment was crucial to the farm's success—more so than comfort of the farmer and his family.

Take a close look at the structures here... and a closer look the next time you wind down a country road.

The scenery will be even more satisfying when you're aware that each barn has a personality all its own.

CLASSIC DUTCH gambrel roof and substantial rain hood are distinctive elements of the basic barn at left. Roof peaks were often extended into "rain hoods" in many designs—these hoods were pointed like the bow of a ship, or blunted and squared.

THREE-STORY RED BARN with an English gambrel roof, above, features contrasting louvered wall openings for ventilation—very typical in Pennsylvania. Louvered openings near the barn roof peaks were known as "wind eyes", from which the word window was derived. The star-shaped openings on this one are a personalized variation.

MASONRY BARN below, located near Paradise, Pennsylvania, has slits for ventilation and a well-built arch above the door. This "bank barn" was built on a slope (bank) so that the farmer can drive up the earthen ramp into the upper level of the barn, where there's space for threshing and storing hay, grain, meal and stock.

FANCY DECORATIONS (lower right) offer a visual treat. These "hex signs" are not superstitious symbols, as is widely believed—they are simply decorations that show the farmer's pride. These signs are popular in "Pennsylvania Dutch Country."

Jerry Irwin

18

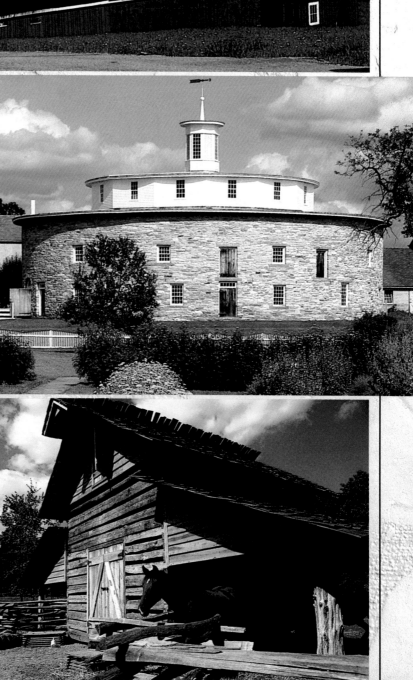

CONTINUOUS ARCHITECTURE. The various sections of the building above, if separated, would be a *cluster* of conventional buildings—barn, milk house, tool shed, woodshed and house. In the parts of New England where the weather is toughest—Maine, Vermont and New Hampshire—this setup sheltered the farmer while doing various chores.

ROUND BARNS such as one at right were briefly popular. This is the Shaker stone barn at Hancock, Mass., built in 1826. It's 270 ft. in circumference, and held 52 head of cattle.

CRIB BARN, lower right, with a center log section and distinctive roof, is typical of the South and Southwest. Since cutting up forage and protecting it from the elements isn't vital there, loft space is usually minimal or nonexistent.

How Will We Tell Duke?

Parents-to-be ponder how they'll break the news to their dog, "Duke" ...he's not going to be an "only child" anymore!

By Bobbi Cain Hershey of Freeport, Illinois

IN JUST a few months, my husband, Todd, and I will have our first baby.

When friends ask whether we feel ready, we nod and flash reassuring smiles. Even though we have no children, we've been "parenting" for 4 years now—ever since the day we got "Duke"!

Anyone looking through Duke's photo album (we call it his "Baby Book") can quickly see that our boy has led a pampered life. We figure he deserved it—before we found him, he'd been dumped in a ditch, taken to the animal shelter, adopted by a neglectful, short-term owner, then returned to the shelter.

On the day I left our farm and went to the shelter, intending to pick out a *small, female puppy,* Duke was just finishing his lunch. One look from his big, dark eyes was all it took. It wasn't his fault he was neither small nor female!

Duke was supposed to be *my* companion. But Todd played rougher and was more tolerant of Duke's shedding coat and huge, muddy paws, so their relationship budded while I stayed safely out of harm's way.

It was soon apparent that Todd really *needed* a dog. After all, a pickup truck is nothing but a machine without a faithful friend in the passenger seat. (Todd decided early that the truck box was too drafty for "his" dog.)

And for Duke, trips to the local grain elevator, to the field and to visit neighboring farmers and *their* spoiled dogs were definitely more fun than traveling to town with Mom in a four-door sedan.

Working Mom's Dilemma

Thanks to Duke, I understand a new mother's mixed feelings about returning to work. Duke was just 3 months old when I was offered a full-time job. He was obviously too young for "group puppy care", but finding a competent baby- (uh, puppy-) sitter at such short notice was a real concern.

Fortunately, Duke's grandma and grandpa (my parents) offered to watch the little guy during my work hours. I dropped him off every morning with his very own blue tote bag, filled with his toys, favorite blue dish and a leash (heaven forbid it should ever be used).

You've heard that having a pet is far less expensive than raising children. I find that hard to believe! Counting puppy and dog food, doctor bills, toys, transportation costs, Halloween costumes and evenings out (yes, Todd's driven 15 miles so that Duke could have soft ice cream in a cone on a hot summer night), our expenses must come close to those of raising a baby.

As any parents would, we found ourselves thinking about our boy's future. I'm sure if there were such things as canine colleges, we'd have Duke enrolled.

We've considered a career in carpentry for Duke. He picks up boards, tools and pencils whenever Todd is mending fence or building something. Trouble is, Duke rarely remembers where he buries the hammer or other tools he carries off.

Spoiled? Yes!

I suppose it's our fault that Duke sometimes sulks and pouts...sneaks into our bed after we're asleep... and talks in a hound voice when he wants to tell us something of vital importance. Maybe it *was* a mistake for Todd to teach this big pal to stand on his hind legs and hug your neck instead of shaking your hand.

But Todd and I can't take all the blame for spoiling Duke. Last Christmas *he* received more presents from family and friends than we did. And lately, friends stop by our house—just to see Duke. We even get letters addressed to him!

Occasionally, I've accused Todd of paying more attention to Duke than to me. And I've scolded Duke for not giving me as much attention, either...after all, I was the one who found him. Still, he always comes to *me* when he has an ache or pain or problem!

But soon I'll be a mom—a *real* mom. I'm looking forward to it. Oh, I realize that family and friends will lavish more attention on the baby than on me, but I'm used to that. It will be kind of nice, though, to be known for a change as the lady with the beautiful baby, instead of "Duke's Mom"!

There's only one worry. How *do* we tell Duke?

Editor's Note: Bobbi has since given birth to a baby boy. She reports that Duke moped around for a few days but is now adjusting to his new "brother"!

Illustration by Jim Sibilski

God's Country

Give me green
rolling hills,
Give me pies cooling
on windowsills...
Give me birds chatting
on telephone poles,
And corn growing midsummer
in patterned rows.
Give me crickets chirping
on warm summer nights,
And children and picnics
and firefly lights...
Give me cows grazing
and sleeping all day,
And children barefooted and tanned
at play.
Give me church socials
and watermelons, please,

And general stores
and swimming holes
and fresh garden peas.
Give me all this,
round the hillside I roam,
And I'll gladly share it all with you
in my country home.

—Barbara Jean Kissel, Cortland, New York

M̲irrored magnificence
is multiplied in Maligne Lake, located southwest
of Alberta, Canada, as the trees of Spirit Island
and the rugged, lavender-tinged Rocky
Mountains reflect in the glassy calm water.
Maligne Lake is in Jasper National Park.
The beauty of this park's majestic jagged
mountains, hot springs and serene lakes makes
it memorable—and a favorite vacation
destination for many.

WHEN I THINK HOW CLOSE

...we came to not finding this place ...this end-of-the-road house in Osage County, Missouri, it scares me.

We were living in Jefferson City then, and the city part was closing in fast. The field across the blacktop from our house was up for sale, all 35 acres. It was ripe and already reeked of "subdivision". The field across our gravel driveway had a "For Sale" sign on it.

So we spent our time every weekend traveling the scenic roads of Osage County—the front seat full of county maps and real estate sheets—looking for a country home. My husband, Bill, and I simply felt Osage County was one of the prettiest spots in Missouri.

Then one sunny morning we found a road we'd missed in all our previous travels. The fact that it ran beside a little creek—Loose Creek—just added to our sense of adventure.

The road led to some beautiful but falling down houses. We stopped at one where a man was working under the hood of his van, and I asked whether he would mind if we looked around and maybe took some pictures. He said to go right ahead and I started to leave...but didn't. And this decision and fraction of a second ended up making all the difference in our lives. Something made me tell him we had been looking for a place of our own in Osage County and how we had been 100% unsuccessful.

The man, who introduced himself as Herbert Haslag, said thoughtfully, "There's a place not too far from here that's been empty for quite a while, but the house still stands sturdy. I'm related to the man who owns the place and I'd be glad to speak to him for you."

He gave us the directions and the excitement began building. We had to go see it. The gravel road was narrow and had a creek-ditch running beside it. When we got to the top of the hill, we turned left on a lane that ran along an oak-lined ridge.

But the best part was when we got to the end of the ridge. The view from there literally made us suck in our breaths! The valley below, the bluff-side creek, the hills folding in on each other, the curving, pine-tree-lined lane going down to the house—what a setting!

And then we saw the house. Oh my! It was the farmhouse we'd been looking for: Large, white, two stories, L-shaped porch, black shutters, guarded by stately shade trees.

It did, indeed, still stand sturdy, as Herbert had promised. There was a white board fence around the outer yard, and there the farm yard had neat blue-painted sheds and a great blue barn set up on stones.

This was *it*, as far as we were concerned. Our search was over...if the owner agreed. We started praying.

Herbert Haslag spoke to the owner, the owner listened, and it was the beginning of our new life in Osage County.

When I think how close we came to not finding this place...this end-of-the-road house in Osage County ...it scares me. But we followed a road that we didn't know was there and—as Robert Frost said—that has made all the difference.

—Rebecca Nunn
Loose Creek, Missouri

Alchemy

Spring caught the sunlight
in a burst of gold,
when today
through rain-swept skies,
and much against its will,
she left it shining
in a bed of daffodil.

—Hattie G. Bowman of Factoryville, Pennsylvania

Dan McWilliams

Blossoming Into Spring!

THE HILLS are alive...with the sounds and scents of springtime!

Warmed by the sun through ever-lengthening days, the countryside awakens and begins its annual burst of floral fancy. Fat buds swell and unfurl into glorious blossoms...fruit trees stretch petal-laden branches and wave them at admirers...meadows spread out carpets of intricate colorful swirls...even deserts and dunes trumpet the season's welcome arrival.

The countryside becomes the Master's palette—a painted backdrop of sprigs, sprays, nosegays and bouquets...each flower nodding to the ooohs and aaahs of springtime enthusiasts.

On the following pages, you'll find photos which capture this sensational show. Turn the pages slowly, from blossom to blossom...you might even smell the fragrance of spring!

WAVES OF WILDFLOWERS billow to the horizon as orange poppies and blue lupines mingle beautifully on a California hillside.

DAISY-DOTTED meadow and New Hampshire's White Mts. make peaceful scene.

Fred Sieb

THISTLE BLOSSOM stopover stills butterfly's wings briefly en route to sweeter things.

26

FourbyFive

Leslie A. Kelly

Deanna Buchanan

ARMFUL OF FLOWERS from Missouri prairie will soon become treasured bouquet for Mom.

FRAGRANT PHLOX (top photo) form purple patch along fence of calm Oregon pond.

STARFLOWER constellation sparkles in the deep-green grass of Louisiana woodland.

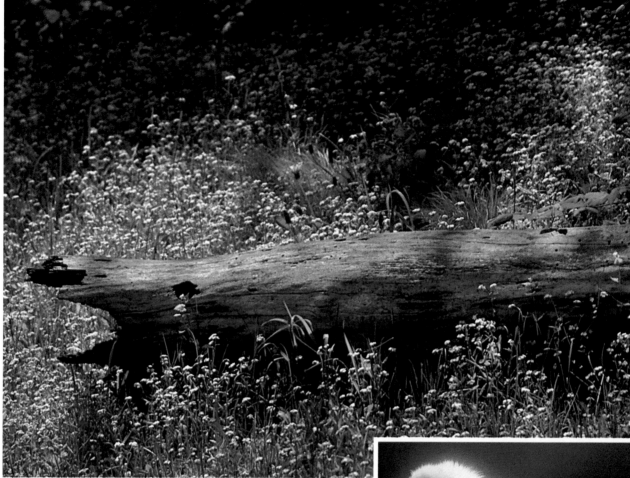

FROTH of flowers billows around a weathered log in Virginia forest, as springtime sun dapples the scene with sunlight and shadow.

BABIES ABOUND as fluffy chicks (right), new-born calves and frisky fillies experience the sun's warmth.

Gene Ahrens

RIPPLED RIDGE of sand dune forms a striking, textured backdrop to golden sunflowers in Great Sand Dunes National Monument of southern Colorado. At right, boy has close encounter of the Dutch kind in Holland, Michigan.

MULEDEER in a flowery Montana meadow is alert yet at ease, lying in a grassy bed.

DEW IS ON THE ROSE in a Washington garden, and across the country (bottom photo), lemon-yellow daylilies and blue lupines nod as green trees form protective backdrop to a lovely New England garden.

Allen Russell

Fred Sieb

E.L. Holland

Philip Ashwood

HAWKSBILL MOUNTAIN (top, left) forms hazy backdrop for delicate mountain flowers in North Carolina.

SCARLET UMBRELLA shelters nature lover (top, center) taking close look at Colorado desert wildflowers.

LILYPADS cover the surface of a Georgia pond (above) with circles of emerald green, accented by waxy purple waterlilies on sturdy stalks.

MOUNTAIN MEADOW (top, facing page) offers colorful invitation to explorers in Grand Teton National Park in Wyoming. Mt. Moran rises to meet the clouds in background.

MUSTARD BLOSSOMS spread a textured yellow carpet beneath apple trees in mid-state New York.

COTTONGRASS ripples in fluffy curves (right) across tundra country of Alaska in front of Mt. McKinley.

GETTING ACQUAINTED, young girl and duckling share a companionable moment in warm spring sun (below).

POPPY PANORAMA will stretch out before you when you turn the page. You'll find yourself in the midst of a flowery field in the majestic Ajo Mountains of Arizona!

David Muench

Somewhere, Over the Rainbow...

B. Christensen/Northwest Photostock

THERE'S something about a rainbow that makes any heart leap a little. Shimmering in the rain-freshened air, its brilliant arcs of color suspended against a clearing sky, a rainbow sparks shouts of "Hey, Mom, look!"

Most children never outgrow it...this lifting of spirits after a thunderstorm.

Most of us commit rainbows only to memory, but the talented photographers whose works appear in this edition committed their favorite rainbows to filmed images to share with you.

Enjoy the jubilee of rainbows on these two pages. These translucent bands of color stretch across varied landscapes...as lingering April raindrops splinter the sunlight into the spectrum of violet, indigo, blue, green, yellow, orange and red...in a foretaste of the colorful May flowers to come.

MARGINAL NOTE: *If at first you don't succeed, try, try a grin.*

B laze of fuchsia flowers
sets off the beauty of Trout Lake,
south of Telluride, Colorado.
Each winter, thousands of people flock to
the deep, powdery snows of the southwestern
part of the state, where once mountain men
traversed the craggy landscape on makeshift skis.
And many more come to enjoy fantastic scenery
such as this, and to soak up the area's frontier
history. As a matter of fact,
Telluride was the scene of Butch Cassidy's
first bank robbery!

'Won't You Be Bored?'

*Moving from the city of Ft. Lauderdale
to the rural wilderness of the Ocala Forest meant some changes
for the writer—firefly congestion replaced traffic jams,
and the calls of whippoorwills and bobwhites replaced horns
and sirens. Her city friends worried she'd be bored
...but a tiny orphan kept her busy!*

◆

BY SONDRA LEE VERDEGEM, FT. MCCOY, FLORIDA

Dogwoods blooming remind me it's time to plant the garden. They also remind me of the dogwood day when one of those little "extras" from the country came into my life.

I was checking out the green sprouts of pepper plants in the flats when the dogs started barking and made a commotion. When I went to see what the trouble was, I found they'd treed a baby squirrel, just a wee one.

I put out my hand, and he held onto my finger and climbed into my palm, showing no fear. He was hungry and thin. The peppers could wait.

Some might question the wisdom of taking in a wild thing, but I promised myself years ago not to hold back when I feel something should be done. The little creature was suffering from lack of food and water, so the first order of business was to nourish him.

I found a small, plastic food coloring bottle, washed it out, filled it with warm milk and squeezed it into his mouth drop by drop. He drank it up with great thirst.

I grabbed every book I could find on squirrels, especially gray squirrels, and quickly read up on the needs of my tree-top ward. By day's end I'd settled on a diet of unsalted pecans, hamster food, new maple leaves, fruit, sunflower seeds and acorns...all of which he squirreled away with gusto. He certainly earned the name my mother gave him: "Mikey", after the little boy in the television commercial who'll eat anything.

Mikey lived in a converted bird cage with dried leaves for carpeting. Dad built a wooden nest box which we attached to one side, and I threw in a holey sweat sock, thinking the little squirrel would like to curl up against it for warmth. Instead, he *wore* it, crawling head first into the ankle hole and peeking out the heel or toe holes.

Each night he'd "hit the sock," rearranging it to suit him. Sometimes he'd take in snacks, like a kid sneaking cookies into bed. Other times, he'd be too lazy to come

out. He'd poke his head through the toe or heel and h[...] tail out the ankle hole and creep—sock and all—to th[...] dish of food or the water bottle, looking like a strange furry turtle!

As Mikey began to grow, his coat got long and slee[...] and his ears and feet got bigger. He remained unafraid— he'd still reach out and touch my hand (he was a left[...] a little southpaw, right from the start).

The bigger he got, the busier he kept me. Sometime[...] as I hustled to fill his needs, I'd laugh to remember [...] friend's concern at my plans to move to the countr[...] "Won't you be bored up there in the forest? There[...] nothing to do!"

Mikey boarded with us for 6 weeks, getting big, f[...] and sassy. He loved his outside-the-cage free time an[...] would romp through the house, running up and dow[...] my arms and legs as though I were a forest tree, the[...] jumping up onto the shades, then to my bookshelves, the[...] over to have his evening snack before finally crawling back into the woolen sock and curling up to go to sleep. As he

38

ew stronger, Mikey's nails would dig into me as he
ayed, and I began to look like the loser in a tangle with
oramble bush. I learned to wear long sleeves and jeans
hen he came out for his romps. If I didn't let him out
play, he'd throw a temper tantrum, tossing leaves, food
shes and sock around in his cage.

Nature always gives us signals, but in this case I was
no hurry to see her message about Mikey. Still, the
gns were obvious—his little teeth could chew through
alnut shells *and* my furniture with equal ease.

"I must set him free," I kept telling myself, and final-
my brain out-reasoned my heart.

The day I set Mikey free, he scampered up the nearest
k, his gray tail flying like a plume behind him. From
high branch he looked over his new world and listened
the song only wild things can hear—or maybe it was
s soul that was singing.

He came back down headfirst and ran toward me, onto stop a few feet away and listen again...he looked
me for a moment, then turned and was gone.

We nailed Mikey's nest box high in the tree, with a
ean sock inside. He used it at first. Every day I put out
od and water, but as time went on, less and less was
ken.

Then one day, I found Mikey's sock on the ground,
ssed aside. I guessed he'd grown up and didn't need
e security of that worn, wooly garment anymore. A few
ays later, a noisy family of blue jays took up residence
Mikey's abandoned box.

I tried to reassure myself that this was all nature's way,
ut worry shaded my thoughts. What if a hawk got
likey...or he wandered trustingly toward a gun-toting
unter? I forced those visions from my head and reminded myself that he'd become an adult, responsible for his
own fate.

Yet a small worry sat on my shoulder, perched where
Mikey once clung...until the day six big squirrels invaded
the yard, romping, playing, stealing food from the bird
feeder.

When I ventured out, all six darted off in different
directions. But then, slowly, one squirrel returned. I held
out my hand, and he cautiously approached.

With a familiar left paw, Mikey touched my world
once again, pausing as I stroked under his chin, closing
his eyes in contentment and making a low, purring sound.
Then his companions called to him, and he scampered
back to the forest, back to his proper place in the order
of things.

Now the transplanted pepper plants stand stoutly in
the soil, putting forth their first fruits. They'll
fight insects, drought and pelting rain, and—
if it is their fate—they'll survive, with a
little help from me.

And as I busy myself in the
garden, I look about at my
country realm and I smile,
recalling my friend's words.
"Won't you be bored?"

Illustration by Jim Sibilski

America's Beautiful...
From Sea to Shining Sea

ACROSS the length and breadth of this land, the scope of country scenery is astounding—rugged seacoasts and placid valleys...dry desert dunes and moist green crops...snow-covered peaks and shadowed streams.

It's all there to be seen, to be appreciated, and to be proud of.

Our photographers' lenses captured these awe-inspiring vistas across the width of America.

Come with us to explore spine-tingling sights stretching from ocean to ocean. And, as you do, reflect on *our* country, and the freedoms and opportunities that are our unique birthright.

This is America the beautiful... and these pictures prove it!

A WAVE-SMOOTHED California beach is bathed in the cloud-rippled, roseate glow of the setting sun as graceful gulls soar above.

Terry Wild/dpi

Fou

OLD GLORY, symbol of our land, people and ideals, waves its colors. Remember their significance? Red for courage and hardiness; blue for vigilance, perseverance and justice; white for purity and innocence.

TOUCHING THE PAST, a young traveler admires the Liberty Bell, which first rang on July 8, 1776, to announce the adoption of the Declaration of Independence. Its timeless inscription reads, "Proclaim liberty throughout the land, to all the inhabitants thereof."

J. Netts/H. Armstrong Roberts

Bill Bridge

RUGGED RIDGES braid at the bottom of the Whitebird Valley in Idaho, while Indian paintbrush plants blaze in the foreground.

NAVAJO RIDER herds his flock across a sandy stretch in front of rock formations in Utah's famed Monument Valley.

D. Muench/H. Armstrong Roberts

CAPTURED CLOUDS dapple a serene stream intersecting verdant, daisy-decked meadow in foothills of northern Arizona.

Doris G. Barker

Randy Jarvis

fpg

FourbyFive

Laastsch-Hupp

SANDSTONE FORMATIONS raise their crenellated columns above Red Rock Crossing, Ariz.

ROCKIES of Glacier Mountain National Park are an impressive sight when viewed from Going-to-the-Sun Road, which crosses the Continental Divide.

WAVES OF WHEAT (far left) break round a wooden windmill—the only vertical object in miles of flat Kansas prairies.

PROUD PATRIOT (near left) celebrates Independence Day with flying colors and serious thoughts, looking very much like a miniature Minuteman in his tricorn hat.

DIFFUSION OF DAYLIGHT filters through California's statuesque redwoods onto flamboyant rhododendrons blooming colorfully in the Redwood National Forest.

Tom Algire/H. Armstrong Roberts

43

Martha Moore

STATELY SYMBOL of freedom and power, a bald eagle alights in its treetop nest.

FLOWING GENTLY through a leafy Michigan glen, stream entertains young hikers.

Phil Dotson/dpi

Ken Dequaine/Third Coast Stock

Dick Smith

WHERE IS EVERYBODY? It must be lunchtime in this peaceful Maine village. Even the pond water is quiet.

WILDFLOWERS (at left) border golden pe oats in Dane County, Wisconsin eld, adding contrasting setting to a trim nd tidy dairy farm in the background.

WAVES LASH at the rocky shores of Bass Harbor Lighthouse in this picture aken along the coast of Maine, completing our photographers' tour across America, from sea (California's coast on page 4) to shining sea (East Coast).

INTERSECTING CRESCENTS of rainbow and foam-edged waves will appear before you when you turn the page, creating geometric arcs at Ecola State Park along the northern Oregon coastline.

Doris Gehrig Barker

Photo following pages: D. Muench/H. Armstrong Roberts

45

A letter from the farm...

By B. Lee Speckels, Ridgecrest, California

Dear Laura,

I'm at my parents' farm in southwestern Missouri as I write this. By the time you read it, I'll be back in California. But for now, at 8 o'clock on a still-light June evening, I can look out the windows and see green, green, green. What a change from the Mojave Desert where I live—everything there is tan, tan, tan!

The peach-colored curtains move away from the window as a refreshing breeze slips into my old upstairs bedroom here on the farm where I grew up. The sky is darkening fast, and thunder is rumbling in the distance. From where I'm sitting, I can see tall walnut and elm trees rustling in the breeze. We'll have a Midwestern-style rain shower shortly—I can feel it in the air.

There have been lightning bugs the last two evenings (I'd almost forgotten about them!). Their little lights flash off and on as they flit across the yard. At night you can hear cicadas, katydids and frogs...and sometimes a pack of coyotes nearby, barking and yelping at the moon.

It's been a long time since I moved away to live in the desert. I was amazed to rediscover just how many different plants and trees there are back in this part of the country. Here, on the edge of the Ozarks, mimosa trees grow wild alongside black walnuts, giant oaks and elms...there are hickory, dogwood, sassafras and more other kinds of trees than I could ever name.

Those trees are filled with birds. This morning I stood on the porch watching them, and I doubt that any aviary could have more variety. Then I remembered that my parents' farm lies in a migratory flight path. Mingled with the many songs of transient birds, I could hear from the permanent residents—the soft coo of mourning doves ...the caw of crows...and the bob-bobwhite of quail.

Later, I went for a walk along the lane, and found that the blackberries are ripe. They're early this year—lucky for me! I had to pick fast, though, 'cause the birds love those berries, too. While picking I spotted a deer in the upper pasture.

There's the shower I predicted—the rain has begun to fall softly now, and I can hear it dripping from the eaves. My old four-poster with its Country Lanes quilt looks especially inviting—it's going to be a great night for sleeping, lulled by the pitter-patter of raindrops.

As I sit here, snug and secure, savoring the sound of softly falling water, my thoughts wander back to similar nights when I was a child. I love this farm, yet circumstances led me far away. How fortunate for me that my parents still live here, that I can visit from time to time. Here I feel safe and secure from the trials and struggles of the world...here where my roots are firmly planted.

It's dark outside now, but my mind's eye can clearly see this big, white, two-storied house that is my refuge. I can envision the lush, green lawn, the shade trees, the wild hay meadow, the pond in the pasture and the old barn loft where I loved to scramble in the hay.

My parents have put in many years of labor on this farm. Now their steps are slower and their backs are bent, but they still love farm life. I'm so glad they've stayed here!

As I lower the window a bit, I take a deep gulp of the fresh, clean, moist air. It clears my mind and my thinking, lifting my reverie and making my soul sing once more.

In a few minutes I'll climb into bed, relax and wiggle my toes against the smooth, white cotton sheets (a favorite thing to do when I was young). And I'll spend my last waking minutes being grateful I still have the farm to come back to.

Thanks to my parents, my own personal Shangri-La lives on, and I'm enjoying it in every pore of my being!

Love, Lee

The stuff that memories are made of...

E.L. Holland

Julie Habel

E.L. Holland

BRING BACK THE OLD 'COUNTRY' PHONE COMPANY!

IF YOU grew up in the country like I did, you have to be as frustrated as I am these days when you place a long distance call.

AT&T *supposedly* tried to make it easier when they changed things so you make a credit card call without the help of an operator. But correctly pushing 25 digits (including the long distance number you're dialing, plus all the digits of your credit card number) is *not* necessarily easier than it was in the old days when we just dealt with a hometown operator.

That fact brings back vivid memories of the day in 1950 when I was a novice seahand aboard a U.S. Navy cruiser. We were based in Philadelphia, a *big* city to me, considering I was just 6 months out of high school and fresh from the plains of South Dakota.

One Friday night in November, we were granted shore leave at the conclusion of a 2-week training cruise. Homesick and seasick, I headed immediately for the row of pay phones that lined every navy dock in those days.

I deposited a carefully preserved nickel (remember?) and dialed "O". Here's a roughly verbatim account of what transpired after the Philadelphia operator answered:

"I'd like to place a station-to-station collect call to the Bob Pence residence in Columbia, South Dakota, please," I said in my best telephone voice.

She was sure she had heard wrong. "You mean Columbia, South CAROLINA, don't you?"

"No, I mean Columbia, South DAKOTA." I had tried to call home once before and I was ready for THAT one.

"Certainly. What is the number, please?" I could tell she still didn't believe me.

"They don't have a number," I mumbled.

The Philadelphia operator was incredulous. "They don't have a *number?*"

"No, ma'am."

"I can't complete the call without a number. Do you have it?" she demanded.

I didn't relish enlarging my role as a country bumpkin, but I knew authority when I heard it. "Well...the only thing I know is...TWO LONGS AND A SHORT."

I think that was the first time she *snorted.* "I'll get the number for you," she said, with an admirable amount of tolerance. "One moment, please."

In deliberate succession, she dialed an operator in Cleveland, who was asked to call one in Chicago, who dialed one in Minneapolis. Then Minneapolis was asked to dial a Sioux City operator, who was asked to ring Sioux Falls, who rang Aberdeen and then—*finally*—Aberdeen rang the operator at my hometown of Columbia.

By this time, Philadelphia's patience was wearing thin. But when Columbia answered, she knew what had to be done.

"The number for the Bob Pence residence, please," Philadelphia said, back in control.

Columbia didn't hesitate an instant. "That's two longs and a short," she responded matter-of-factly.

Philadelphia was obviously stunned, but she plowed on. "I have a collect call from Philadelphia, Pennsylvania, for anyone at that NUMBER. Will you please ring?"

Again Columbia didn't miss a beat. "They are not home."

Philadelphia paused to digest this. She didn't want to set herself up again, so she relayed the message to me that I'd already heard: "There is no one at that NUMBER. Would you like to try again LATER?" no doubt hoping her shift would soon end.

Columbia quickly interrupted: "Is that you, Dick?"

"Yeah, Margaret. Where are the folks?"

Philadelphia was baffled, but she knew she had to look out for the company. "Sir...madam...you can't talk..."

Columbia paid no mind. "They're up to the schoolhouse at the basketball game. Want me to ring?"

I knew I was on real thin ice with Philadelphia, so I said, "It's probably too much trouble."

Philadelphia was still in there trying to protect the company. By this time, though, she was out of words. "But ...but..." she stammered.

Columbia was oblivious. "No trouble at all, Dick. It's halftime." My nickel was still in the phone and I didn't want to start over, so I caved in. "All right."

Mustering her most official tone, Philadelphia made one last effort: "This is a *station-to-station* collect call!"

"That's all right, honey," said Columbia. "I'll just put it on Bob's bill."

Philadelphia was still protesting when the phone rang and was answered at the schoolhouse.

"I have a station-to-station call for Bob Pence," Philadelphia said, by now realizing that somehow Ma Bell may have been bested.

"This is he," said the answering voice.

Philadelphia gave up. "Go ahead."

I'm glad I couldn't see her face when I began my end of the conversation the way all country folks do. "Hi, Dad. How's the weather?"

"Humph!" Philadelphia said, then clicked off the line.

I don't like to think about it, but AT&T no doubt began to automate its long-distance service the next Monday morning. And now look where we are.

—*By Richard Pence of Fairfax, Virginia*

Illustration by Jim Sibilski

Here's to Horses!

COUNTRY would not be "country" without horses. In the 5,000 years since man and horse first teamed up, horses have provided much more than mere horsepower. These noble, intelligent animals have been man's companions, co-workers, "recreational vehicles" and "scenery enhancers". They still hold those jobs to this day.

Equine grace and strength is readily evident in this photographic salute to horses. Draft horses strain in harness and show what *real* horsepower is...cow ponies nimbly cut cattle from the herd or bring a straggler back into the ranks... Morgan mare and foal frolic (upper right)...a fuzzy foal basks in the morning sun...and (far lower right) three high-spirited beauties race off with tails bannering.

It isn't often you see a herd of horses as large as the one at far right, where they fan out across Colorado rangeland on their way up the mountains to summer pasture.

Why not study these pictures and, for a minute, take a mind's ride... gallop along a beach... through a stream...across the country...with the air in your hair and the sun on your back? Imagine riding across a meadow, with your best horse beneath you and your best friend beside. Welcome to the country!

If you love horses, you are not alone. There are 5.25 million horses in the U.S., with 378,000 in Texas and 389,000 in California. Over 27 million Americans saddle up to ride—more than half of them on a regular basis.

So, here's to horses! We salute them for the pleasure they bring us... we'd bring each of them a carrot if we could!

T.

Mack & Betty Kelley

FourbyFive

ontrasting colors and
textures of deep blue sky, green brush and
striated, surrealistically shaped red-gold rocks
create an intricate, interesting panorama
in Monument Valley.
Shared by Arizona and Utah, this region
includes fantastic shapes first formed by the
earth's upheaval and volcanic eruption, then
sculpted by wind, rain and sun.
Spider Rock, Totem Pole, the Three Sisters and
the Left and Right Mitten formations
are just a few of the "Monuments"
rising from the expanse of sand.

Listen to the Trees Sing

By Burl N. Corbett of Birdsboro, Pennsylvania

ON A SUNNY Sunday afternoon recently, I took my two young daughters "catfishing".

Now, those girls have no more interest in catching catfish than I have in shooting an elephant. But the day was warm and lovely, and keeping these two little girls and their daddy indoors would have been as difficult as stopping the river's flow.

The river—the Schuylkill River in southeastern Pennsylvania—flowed indeed, and we sat for 2 hours watching it and wondering where the catfish were.

Actually, catching fish would have been a drawback; little girls would rather throw sticks and rocks in the water, and they think catfish are "gross", anyway.

When the girls' barrage of sticks threatened to entangle the lines I'd stretched patiently into the water, I enticed them to sit quietly with bribes of orange soda from the 5-gallon bucket that serves triple duty as cooler, seat for daddy and fish-transfer device.

(A great many of the fish I catch when fishing with my daughters are taken home alive, then released in the small brook that flows through our farm. My daughters want to "see what they do"—and what they do, of course, is promptly head downstream back in the direction of the Schuylkill River!)

Moving water has charms to soothe the savage beast— and even little girls. For a time, they sipped their sodas and watched the river flow. The day was sunny, with white clouds scudding in a southerly wind, and before long, 5-year-old Heather said, "I can see clouds in the water, Daddy."

Not to be outdone, Amber, 7, said, "I see trees in the water, too." I waited for the inevitable question:

"Why are the clouds in the water, Daddy?" Heather asked.

"They aren't really in the water," I answered. "Just their reflections."

Amber, 2 years older and *infinitely* wiser, nodded.

"The water's like a mirror. Right, Daddy?"

"That's right," I said. I could see that Heather wasn't convinced. *After all,* she probably thought, *if catfish can live in the water, why can't clouds?*

And though I was beginning to doubt that catfish *did* live in the water, not having had a bite, I could see her point. It was no more a miracle for clouds to be in the water than in the sky.

Pondering the unlikely trinity of clouds, water and catfish, we sat quietly and watched our lines slanting into the clouds and sycamores shimmering atop the water.

Soon, the girls finished their sodas. But before they were compelled to start throwing sticks once more, a tree sang to us.

"What's that noise?" Amber asked, peering upward.

The spreading sycamore above us, limbs festooned with remnants of lines from errant casts, was rubbing against a neighboring elm in the wind, like bow against fiddle.

"The tree is singing to us," I replied.

"Trees can't sing," Amber scoffed with the assurance of a girl too big and smart to be fooled by her daddy.

"Sure they can," I said. "Just listen and you'll hear it again."

Amber frowned. "It's just creaking in the wind," she said, stomping off to throw sticks.

But Heather stared seriously into the intermingled web of branches, and I knew that to her still-innocent ears, the tree *was* singing...and in her eyes the clouds *were* swimming. In her heart, the world was alive, as it once was for us all.

But soon she lost interest in singing trees and went back to throwing sticks. And the day came a little closer when the world would lose its magic for her.

As I watched my girls running up and down the bank, laughing and shouting, I hoped that day of lost magic would never come for Heather. There are a few of us who still see the world as freshly as when we were young and othing was impossible—not even singing trees.

The trees have always sung to me, because I have
always listened. Sometimes the song has been but a
whisper—evergreens sing in those hushed tones. Other
times, in a winter gale, the song has been harsh, dissonant
and punctuated by cracking and snapping—lightning-
damaged oaks know this song well.

In the summer, trees' songs are sometimes drowned out
by insects, great singers themselves. But the tree-songs
are still there, faint and constant, ebbing and flowing.

During autumn, the random rustling of falling leaves
accompanies the trees in their annual roundelay of wistful
regret, as they sing farewell to summer's glories.

And in winter, elbow-patches of snow on bare limbs
add emotional power to the trees' sad and lonely dirges,
reverberating up and down the frostbound mountains.

In spring, amid the quacking of mating frogs, I hear
the trees sing once again the familiar and welcome ode
to life and birth.

I thought of all these songs as I watched my daughters
play and watched our fishing rods, motionless against the
water-clouds. Then a small bass jumped, and the clouds
dissolved in a spreading circle of impressionistic light. The
sun went behind a sky-cloud, and the wind turned chill. I
reeled in the lines and called to my girls.

On the drive home, I asked them if they liked the river.
Amber said no, but I knew better. Heather said yes.

"What did you like best?" I asked her.

"The clouds in the water."

I nodded. "I liked the trees singing to us, too," I said.

"Trees don't sing, Daddy," Amber insisted.

But I know better. And I think Heather does, too.

Illustration by Jim Sibilski

Country Brooks, Foaming Falls, Placid Ponds...
Awash with Beauty

WHAT'S there about water that has a mesmerizing effect? No one seems to know, but it's there. Even when you can't see it, a trickling stream, "Z"-ing down a country hillside, takes tension out of your shoulders and slows your pulse rate.

For this issue, our roaming photographers captured the wonders of rural waterways—from quiet creeks to hidden falls to pasture pools—in pictures so perfect you'll feel you're *there.*

On these two pages and those that follow, let your imagination go as you admire silk-smooth water-polished stones...feel the tickle of minnows against your ankles as you wade in a cool creek...the tug of the line as a trout dances on a mountain stream.

Shoes 'n socks off? Pants legs rolled up? Good. Now join us for a trip down country waterways!

SHOWY ACCENTS to nature's decor, tiger lilies glow against the frothy backdrop of cascading Burney Falls in northern California.

WATER-WORN ROCK steers stream, a soft gray contrast to the blue of a Colorado creek.

Mack & Betty Kelley

Scott Spiker

Thomas Kitchen/Tom Stack & Associates

CATTAIL BOG surrounds a camouflaged fisherwoman trying her luck in Idaho stream.

MEANDERING CREEK (top) zig-zags quietly through Great Smokies National Park, Tenn.

VERDANT CARPET covers every surface in Hoh Rain Forest of far northwest Washington.

TRIPPING over rocky terraces in a wooded cove, Colorado's Paige Boulder Creek is framed by greens in variegated shades and soft textures.

JADE-GREEN grass (top left) forms glistening overhang to shimmering silver water in Grand Teton wetlands.

EVER see water clearer than this? Opaque falls rush over rounded rocks of Cosby Creek in Tennessee woods.

PARABOLA of fly line frames fisherman hip-boot-deep in his element, casting in quest of the elusive "Big one."

BUTTERCUPS spread liberally across grassy meadow (right), bordering a tumbling Southwestern rural stream.

Louis Borie/Photo/Nats

The Stock Market

Rod Planck/Tom Stack & Associates

Vinyard Bros. Photo

Joe Cole

Louis Borie/Photo/Nats

UNDERWATER WEEDS weave a striated pattern in between fern-bordered banks of Michigan's Butternut Creek.

RIVERSIDE recreation abounds at the natural playground of the White River near Rochester, Vermont—fishing, wading, picnicking, sunning and just "sitting a spell".

KINGFISHER (far left) rests for a moment after a successful dive, its patient stream-side vigil richly rewarded with fresh crayfish snack.

PERCHED on a boulder, a swimmer takes a break at the foot of Turner Falls in Oklahoma, momentarily hypnotized by water's motion as it slides and splatters over rugged rock wall.

SUNSET on Idaho's Salmon River dyes water pink as it swirls past jutting sandbars and sweeps around the angles and bends.

BUFFALO STILL ROAM on western Montana's National Bison Range, as you'll see when you turn the page. The Flathead River meanders lazily through the valley of this 19,000-acre big game area, established in 1908. Over 400 bison graze these grasslands.

Bill Bridge/dpi

Illustration by Jim Sibilski

...Western-Style

By Jay Simons of Noxon, Montana

IT WAS dry and hot—the good, penetrating kind of heat that cures hay in a hurry...and makes haying miserable.

My 6-year-old son, Ben, filled a gallon jug with cool spring water while daughter Rina, 15, packed some fruit and granola bars. Then we jumped in the pickup and bumped down the dusty gravel road to our neighbor's hay field.

I drove to the far edge, where there were fresh bales on the ground, and we began the prickly, hot and exhausting job of hefting and stacking them in the pickup. The first load didn't take long. Soon we were headed up the mountain to unload and restack the bales in our old barn.

The horse and cows looked up when we passed, and when they smelled the aroma of fresh-mown hay, they whinnied and mooed and pawed the ground. I stopped when a sympathetic Rina said, "Wait, Mom—I'll break open a bale and throw them a bit."

We unloaded and stacked without stopping for a break. It was early in the day; our muscles were handling the task with no complaints, and our thirst was easily slaked by the now-lukewarm jug. Ben got a refill before we headed back for another load.

Each trip took a little longer. The sun baked through our wide-brimmed hats and the long-sleeved shirts we wore to protect ourselves from the sun and chaff. *Perhaps we'll make this do for today,* I thought after the fourth trip, now feeling tired and sore.

But I knew it would take 200 bales to feed our animals over winter. "Maybe one more load," I told the kids, surveying the bales dotting the undulating landscape.

The sun burned hotter. There were no clouds or trees to offer relief. An apple, granola bar and drink of now-hot water in the scant shade of the pickup renewed our spirits...but the flesh was weakening.

Hoping to save another trip, we stacked the bales precariously high and tied them down with twine. "Think you'll make it up the mountain with that load?" the rancher asked, eyeing our top-heavy burden as we pulled away.

"We'll make it," I assured him, at the same time giv-ing my daughter the order, "Keep an eye on the bales."

The springs groaned and creaked as we inched back to our road. I shifted into low gear and crept, mound by mound, rivulet by rivulet, rock by rock, up the steep incline to our homestead. Halfway there, Rina gasped. "Watch it, Mom—it's *wobbling!*"

I slowed, but too late...the bales began to shift, then slide. "It's *going*, Mom!" Rina wailed. "Oh, no, we've lost half the load!"

I pulled into the turnout, where the pickup would be out of the way of logging trucks. Sighing, I dusted off my hat and grabbed my gloves.

It was 2 hours later when we finally straggled into our lane. "Forget about unloading this batch till morning," I said. "It can stay on the truck overnight."

"Can we go down to the lake and take a swim?" Rina asked hopefully. I nodded. "You kids go ahead," I replied. "And take your time, okay?"

I sat at the wheel of the pickup, beads of perspiration dripping from my nose. The sun had moved into the western sky and the mountains had turned blue. The cabin, silhouetted against the tree line, seemed a continent away.

A bird fluttered from a ponderosa pine and perched on the rim of the livestock tank at the edge of the pasture. I watched it for a moment, then, wobbly-legged, climbed down and walked toward the tank, peeling off my sweaty, dusty clothes as I went.

The sun had been beating down on that water all day long, and it was almost too hot to bear as I slid down into it, dunking my head, blowing out bubbles and coming up with my hair plastered to my closed eyelids.

The scolding of a pine squirrel opened my eyes to a peaceful scene—aspens and pines bordering the grassy meadow where our white horse stood, regarding me quizzically.

No Roman empress could ever have had a more satisfying bath. I grinned as the day's weariness began to ease away. *You can keep your castles,* I thought with a slow shake of my head. *I'll take country—and a cow tank on a mountaintop—anytime!*

Country Roads

A day spent walking country roads
Offers so many things—
The beauty of a buttercup,
The joy a rainbow brings...

Soft music of a singing bird,
Movement of a grazing herd,
Blue cloudless skies and swaying trees,
Green rolling hills, a soothing breeze...

All these combine to ease from mind
The daily worries, words unkind;
Summer sun setting in bands of gold,
Lightens the heart, revives the soul.

Teri DeBlieck, Gerlaw, Illinois

Photo/Nats

Country Canvases

THE POETIC PATTERNS of rural America often escape the ground-level observer. So our *Country* photographers rose to lofty heights to capture the country contours here and on the next two pages.

These pleasing vistas let you enjoy the striking "geo-graphics" that result when the earth is the canvas, crops are the palette and an unassuming farmer is the artist. So, c'mon...soar with us for awhile over these country canvases and savor the sights!

There, at the right, see the neatly mitered corners of the Kansas wheat field as it's being combined? And down there in Alabama, see that wedge of cotton pickers leaving mattress-ticking stripes in their wake? Count 'em...I get 32 of them.

Look! Look over there in Illinois...see the graceful, parabolic sweep of those Illinois soybean plants? And there in Ohio, the crazy quilt of ripening and harvested crops next to lush meadows and stitches of streams and fence rows?

Now look out West...see the sinuous waves of wheat contrasting with newly plowed ground in Washington's fertile Palouse Valley? And directly below, note the delineated squares of Iowa farmland, dappled with cloud shadows.

Isn't this a neat experience? There's more...stay aboard as we soar over more scenes on the next two pages...

Comstock

Gene Ahrens/

Peter Menzel/Atlas Image

Concord/Xio

Johnson/Xio

OH, WOW…is this a super scene or what? I hope the family that lives on that Illinois farm at left has flown over their place to see this.

And look up there at those softly mounded parallel rows of soybeans, dipping across a Wisconsin field…and below us, at that Missouri farmer painting dark stripes with his combine as he harvests corn.

Oh, isn't *that* something? Look at those grapevines standing in ranks in that California vineyard …and those alternating sweeps of corn and wheat mingling summer colors in Minnesota.

Hey *look!* That's *us!* Somebody took a picture of our plane as we soared over that Louisiana rice paddy at left! See our shadow on the levee?

Hasn't this been a great trip? Want to do it again? Good. Keep looking and soaring long as you'd like!

ily pads mingle with reflection-captured clouds on the smooth surface of Little Molas Lake, near Silverton in the rugged San Juan Mountains of southwest Colorado. Colorful history pervades this area, including the background of the name of Silverton: Legend has it that an early miner once remarked, "We may not have any gold here, but we have silver by the ton!" And the Million Dollar Highway runs between Ouray and Silverton—a portion of U.S. 550 that's surfaced in low grade gold ore, a stretch that's said to give travelers a million-dollar view.

City gal who can't ride observes more than the broncs and the bulls while sitting on a blanket on a hill, taking in the Killdeer Mountain Rodeo.

Hometown Rodeo Is Slice of Rural Life

By Jane Greer

THERE'S a sad little cluster of peeling white bleachers, but since they face directly into the sun, most locals elect to sit on a blanket on the hillside opposite, where the view is great in spite of the dust.

To keep the blowing grit down, a tractor and sprayer work the arena to a perfect moistness; children in battered Stetsons and their best boots hug the fence and squawk in pleasure when the wind blows the spray at them.

Killdeer, North Dakota, population 790, clings to a curve on ND 22 just above ND 200. The Killdeer Mountains, north and west of town, once site of a near-bloodless Army-Indian battle, rise incongruously from the clear plain, a dark reminder that anything is possible.

One can drive around the mountains in about half an hour, climb them in 15 minutes, and from the top see forever across mildly rolling grasslands and chest-high wheat, hazy in the heat. Only 150 miles from the Canadian border, Killdeer nonetheless acknowledges mainly the "west" in "Midwest."

At 2:00 exactly, a stunning, wide-nostrilled buckskin carrying an even more stunning blonde (red boots, red hat, white satin shirt, red satin pants) prances into the arena and then breaks into an easy lope. She's "Miss Rodeo North Dakota", the buckskin just another taut, obedient part of her body.

Two Points of View

Most men would stand to see her better, and some men to see her horse; all the men here, and the women with them, stand because Miss Rodeo North Dakota bears the American flag, its pole tucked neatly into the top of her right boot. She circles twice, then reins up slightly east of center. Behind her are two horsemen with the state and rodeo association flags.

A local woman will sing our national anthem. I expect the worst and am gratified and surprised: Her voice is confident, tone-true, rich and shim-

Larry Sanders/Western Exposure

"The action's fast...the riders are rugged...and the people in the stands are *real.*"

MARGINAL NOTE: It's what you learn after you know it all that counts.

nery, what city folks call "country-western". No one fools around or talks or opens a Coke or a beer; all eyes are straight ahead, all hands over a heart. We applaud after the anthem, and then the arena clears.

Sitting on a blanket on the hill, we are surrounded by solid, youngish men with farmer tans and hard arms, older, rounder men in string ties, women in tank tops or chambray shirts tucked into tight jeans.

My husband's 5-year-old nephew is with us, determined to hate the rodeo. (He changes his mind before it's over.) Steven looks silly in a blue surfer shirt and shorts, sandals, and sunglasses, surrounded by kids in down-at-the-heels Tony Lamas and serious-looking dark felt hats.

What will happen first? he wonders. *Calf roping,* his mother says. *Cat roping?* he asks, only mildly interested, and we all laugh a little self-consciously.

After every calf-roping contestant Miss Rodeo North Dakota's dazzling buckskin bulldogs the calves back to their pen. The duo are not a mere showpiece. In every event, the home-town boys get a big hand—the announcer asks for it, but he wouldn't

have to—regardless of how they score.

Several bowlegged teenagers in snug jeans and chaps fail to stay on their broncs; they're local heroes, headed for the Nationals later in the summer, and toe the dust and blush when we applaud their good tries.

Outlanders get applause, too, for nice rides on broncs or bulls or winning times wrestling their steers to the ground. So do horses who outwit their riders (the livestock racks up points for orneriness and grit just like the human contestants do).

Let's hear it for Todd Splonskowski, ladies and gentlemen—he's one of the best, and he gave it everything he's got. And while you're at it, let's give a big hand to Old Ironsides. He had a job to do and he done it. Todd limps out, and Old Ironsides ditches the pick-up men for one last spry two-step around the fence.

Partial to Horses

The smart cowponies, who, with or without a rider, can counter every move a calf or steer might dream up, draw admiration from the announcer and the crowd, but the bovine stock isn't given much credit.

I've seen a wily, ring-wise little calf outwit a big man on a horse, though,

by hightailing it to the far end of the arena and then sliding *under* the gate to mama, slick as Lou Brock stealing home. *Everybody* comes here to work.

There is some money to be won, but not a lot, especially after gas and feed and entry fee bite into it. It's hard to think of a harder way to make a dollar. This is North Dakota's oldest rodeo, but not a particularly big one, yet there are riders up here from Iowa and Kansas, Wyoming and even Texas; these fellas aren't hobbyists.

Riders on the Move

Each one will stay on that bull or get thrown, loop that calf or lose him, flip that steer or miss by a hair and fall open-mouthed into the dirt at 30 miles an hour—and then pick up his crushed hat, dust himself off, amble to the trailer, pack it all up, and drive 30 miles south to Dickinson for *that* rodeo 3 hours from now. Tomorrow it's South Dakota, maybe, or Montana.

I never go to a rodeo without some dread; softhearted about animals. I didn't grow up *using* them. Always in the back of my brain is the fear that I'll watch a horse break a leg or see a calf's neck shattered by his own speed after being thrown. (I'd hate to see a hurt cowboy, too, of course, but part of me figures they ask for it.)

Still, there is an aspect of surprise pain in real life, and what these guys do in the ring (aside from bull-riding and wild-cow milking), they and other men do every day because they *must,* with much more to lose and less to win. There are still parts of life that can't be computerized.

So here I sit, a city girl who can't even ride...feeling suddenly, strangely self-satisfied.

There's no special moral to this tale, except that maybe Heaven *isn't* a hammock in the shade. What's here is immediate, strenuous, *authentic.*

Old Glory snaps over the announcer's booth in the harsh plains wind. Tonight there will be firecrackers, and watermelon, and a room full of people who love me; and tomorrow in the shadow of the distant, improbable Killdeer Mountains, anything is possible.

—Reprinted from *CHRONICLES: A Magazine of American Culture,* published by The Rockford Institute.

No ticket needed...join us for a walk through
Autumn's Outdoor Art Gallery!

AUTUMN'S ARTISTRY can take your breath away. You look left or right, and your eyes catch canvases so colorful you want to commit them to memory.

You'd like to say something profound to describe these outdoor paintings, but all you hear coming from your lips again and again is an appreciative "oooh!"

Dipping a brush into a wide-ranging palette of vivid hues, the Master Artist prepared this private show with a lavish hand. Yet the brush strokes are not always broad... some are in soothing subtle styles.

Consider the still life below of autumn's bounty...the impressionistic canvas of the misty morning at right...the art nouveau effect of a scarlet vine climbing a gray tree...the abstract splash of one flamboyant hardwood waving gaudily from a grove of pines.

These paintings will soon be on display across America. For a preview, let your fingers do the walking through the following pages.

Bill Ross/West Light

Joel Baldwin/The Stock Market

74

UBTLE SHADINGS and lines softened
y mist make a golden monochrome of
illy Indiana corn field, where handcut
hocks dot the land like silent sentries.

APING THE REWARDS of gardening,
impressive pile of produce (at far left)
eates an intensely colorful still life.

ROZEN MOMENT captures floating
ber leaves and youthful fall fun in Illi-
is meadow. You can sense the exuber-
ce inspired by crisp, cool October air.

IE BROAD STROKES of saffron-yellow
pens form vivid counterpoint to the
pre subtle shading of the hillside ever-
eens at Dolores Canyon in Colorado.

BUSHEL BASKET becomes a leafy
for feline enjoying an Indian summer
At right, grandpa and granddaughter
forces to create a special jack-o-lan
out of a pumpkin they picked toget

RAINY ROAD, far right, gleams a
wends its way through abstract pat
of black tree trunks and glowing lea

SILVERY-BLUE Chapel Pond (lower
forms a shimmering backdrop to birc
in the Adirondacks of upstate New Y

DAPPLING of red-orange foliage is
off by the deep-green spikes of ev
greens in this rugged Utah landsca

Fred Sieb

Roger A. Kingsford/Laatsch-Hupp

Laatsch-Hupp

H. Abernathy/H. Armstrong Roberts

MULTI-HUED, multi-textured brocade of early fall colors is draped in rich folds across his Missouri landscape, as post-storm light breaks across he horizon and highlights a weathered barn in foreground.

VEIL OF MIST hangs in the air, softening this New Hampshire scene, where a weathered split rail fence meandering along a clay gravel road sets off the deep red plumes of maple trees.

REFLECTIONS form green-yellow bands across the Buffalo River in Arkansas, backed by the subtly hued striated rock formation of the bluffs.

W. McKinney/H. Armstrong Roberts

VETY GREEN of this New York mea-
* sets off the yellow leaves of a wide-
spreading oak tree (left). Above, an
t-point buck surveys its surroundings.

Dick Dietrich

MAJESTIC BACKDROP of Mt. Sneffels rises to meet the clouds in this dramatic Colorado landscape, where aspens, evergreens alternate to create contrasts.

PLACID POOL formed behind beaver's dam mirrors upright trunks of birch and pine. Unseen beavers are busy below storing winter food!

VILLAGE VISTA captures contented Holsteins at edge of tiny town in Northeast; typical New England church steeple adds just the right accent to placid scene.

PANORAMIC PATCHWORK will spread before you when you turn the page, as glorious view of neatly fenced farmland near Peacham, Vermont comes into sight, colored by bold brush of autumn's artistry.

J. Gleiter/H. Armstrong Roberts

Shhh...I Hear the Country Calling

By Mary Ellen Pourchot, Neshkoro, Wisconsin

"ISN'T IT awfully *quiet* in the country?"

"What will you *do* all day?"

Those were questions friends asked on the spring day we told them we were moving to rural Wisconsin. I didn't admit it then, but I, too, wondered if I could adjust to the country after living in the city all my life.

Now, months later, I'm still adjusting...not to what I miss of the city, but to the wonder of each day's discoveries here in the country.

My first discovery was that the country is *not* quiet. It seemed so at first, when my ears were still accustomed to loud city noises. But now that I've learned to listen through the country's silence, I hear a wonderful symphony of natural sounds.

We've traded the honking of car horns for the faraway honking of Canada geese, their wings pumping, long black necks stretched southward. Our new home is right under their flyway, and we never tire of watching them wing overhead, stirring the air with their annual migration music.

Watching one afternoon recently, we saw one forlorn bird drop from the line, drift to our lake and settle on the bay. His squawks told of weariness.

Suddenly another goose swerved out of the line, changed course, and headed back. He skimmed the water and honked encouragement to the drop-out. We wanted to cheer when, at last, the tired goose flapped its wings, pedaled across the water's surface, and rose to continue his journey southward. I feel sorry for our city friends who miss such slices of nature's drama.

Other surprises come when we walk our land and listen to its sounds. In spring we hear a far-off *put-put-put* in the woods and think someone is trying to start up an old tractor. A country neighbor, smiling, explains: "That's the courting ritual of the ruffled grouse. The drumming sound you think is a tractor comes when he beats his wings against the air."

Some country sounds can barely be heard. On a cold November morning we walk through the woods in new snow that muffles every step. It is so still we feel we might be the only ones out...but then we read in the snow the tell-tale signs of others who have been here. The eyelet tracks of a rabbit embroider the lane...feathered lines mark the activity of field mice under berry briars...and heart-shaped tracks lead us to a patch swept clear of snow, where deer have bedded.

Returning quietly to the house against a winter sun that casts a pink glow on the snow, we hear a rustle of brush and catch a sudden glimpse of a long, red-brown animal at the edge of the woods. It's a red fox! It pauses for one perilous moment, twitches a bushy tail, then slips noiselessly away.

We treasure that one unexpected sighting more than a dozen trips to some crowded city zoo.

Nothing to do? Hardly. Too quiet?

Not at all. As our senses—once deadened by city smog and traffic clatter—awaken to our environment, we begin to tune in to the sounds and sights and scents that enrich country living. And our heightened senses make every morning an awakening to new discoveries.

Autumn Panorama

Saucy red squirrels gather their winter hoard,
And dart among the crunchy leaves,
That slowly drift earthward, one by one.

Honking wild geese now southward bent
Fly low along the margin of the lake,
Or linger in the waters at its brink.

Warm and dreamy Indian summer sun
Touches hazy vapors floating by,
And freckles them with red-gold glow.

The play of moonlight, pale and white,
Glimmers on crinkly corn shocks at wood's edge,
And wraiths of Indian campfires hover near.

The flaming panorama closes now,
As all the richly bedaubed leaves of fall
Scatter with the first breath of winter's wind.

—*Margaret Dillon of Janesville, Wisconsin*

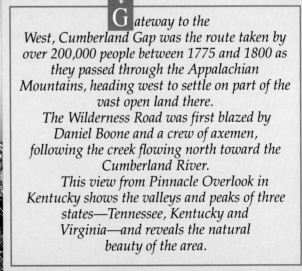

*G*ateway to the
*West, Cumberland Gap was the route taken by
over 200,000 people between 1775 and 1800 as
they passed through the Appalachian
Mountains, heading west to settle on part of the
vast open land there.*
*The Wilderness Road was first blazed by
Daniel Boone and a crew of axemen,
following the creek flowing north toward the
Cumberland River.*
*This view from Pinnacle Overlook in
Kentucky shows the valleys and peaks of three
states—Tennessee, Kentucky and
Virginia—and reveals the natural
beauty of the area.*

Walk Through Our Winter Wonderland.

Ken Dequaine

WISCONSIN WINTER embellishes this farm scene as the heavy snow bends down every branch.

GOT A PENCIL? Take this dow
Start with a flash of icy beauty
add two deep breaths of pine sme
...mix in an abundance of holid
tastes...top it off with a frosting
white snow...that's the recipe fo
magical potpourri called "winte

While the season's first blast m
send the faint-hearted indoors, t
brave love it brisk! They enjoy t
glow of chill-reddened cheeks
the exhilaration of cold outdoor a
tivities...the sights, scents ar
sounds of a white-washed worl

Back indoors, they like bei
warmed by a mug of hot cocoa
crackling fire, a woolen afghan
and enjoy the slower pace wi
family and friends.

Our rural photographers brav
the elements to capture winte
arrival across the country. Cor
along, enjoy the views...you do
have to bundle up for this trip!

WHITE-GOLD GLOW punctuates evergre
festoons looping their festive way along
fenceline and around the silo on this holid
bedecked farm near Ann Arbor, Michiga

H.G. Ross/H. Armstrong Roberts

HOARFROST adds velvety texture and subtle new dimension to this bird's-eye view of a cold cluster of pine cone and needles.

BRINGING IN THE TREE, Idaho cowboy returns to his rustic cabin with pine carefully selected and cut from nearby forest, soon to be decorated by his eagerly awaiting family.

PATCH OF YELLOW aspens creates a pleasing contrast to the evergreens whitened by early snow that caught them by surprise, in this Colorado scene set off by an azure sky.

H. Armstrong Roberts

M. Uselmann/H. Armstrong Roberts

COTTONY TUFTS of snow highlig
this secluded landscape near Bue
Vista, California, defining the spea
of evergreens and arcs of the shrub

SMOOTH SLEDDING is the order
the day for this trio of passenge
(above right), sliding down serer
main street of a New England villag

EXHILARATING RIDE blushes th
cheeks of these riders as they gallc
headlong across a snowy field, chille
by the air, yet warmed by the exercis

COTTON CANDY COVERING of w
snow transforms Wasatch Mountair
near Salt Lake City, Utah, into so-quie
you-could-hear-a-pin-drop landscap

90

CLOSE-UP VIEWS of winter show bright-eyed junco enjoying some sunshine; and the intense jewel-hued combination of emerald and ruby meeting in a holly bush.

A MIXTURE OF EMOTIONS rides toboggan as boy grins with glee, puppy seeks escape.

FROTHY RUSH of water leaves its icic autograph on banks of New Jersey strea while dun and scarlet female cardinal (le proudly poses on her snowy look-out perc

KANSAS LANDSCAPE'S stark beauty softened by frosting of a morning snowfa

SPUN-SUGAR COATING disguises rugg landscape (above right), as whipped crea dollops mask the granite rocks underneat

AWASH IN MOONLIGHT, snowdecked sce takes on a surrealistic, blue-tinged radianc

Leonard Lee Rue III/dpi

CONSIDERING THE SITUATION, a red fox stops at forest's edge. And when you turn the page, the warm glow of lights will add golden accents to a wintery evening view of the much-photographed village of East Corinth, Vermont.

Zefa/H. Armstrong Roberts

93

Doris Gehrig Barker

I had driven to our small cabin up in the north woods with my dog, "Natasha", to get away from the holiday rush for a day. Not too long after I arrived, I found myself completely snowed in—on Christmas Eve!

A call home confirmed that the roads were impassable. Promising my husband, Tom, and our girls I'd be there as

The Cardinal Tree

By Sharma Krauskopf
Lansing, Michigan

soon as the plow got through, I resolved to make the best of things. After all, our small cabin had electricity, a dependable wood stove, lanterns and plenty of food. Spending the night was clearly better than taking the chance of becoming stranded on a blizzard-bound highway.

Still, it didn't take long for loneliness to set in. I knew the best defense was to keep busy, so I set about decorating the cabin...after all, it *was* Christmas Eve!

I bundled up, waded out into the storm, and quickly cut a short, fat pine. Back in the cabin, with my Christmas tree thawing near the stove, I foraged for holiday trappings.

I began making plans for a personal Christmas Eve dinner: roast chicken, canned peas, potatoes, gravy and an apple pie. As I peeled apples for the pie, I hummed along to Christmas carols on the radio.

With the pie in the oven, I turned my attention to trimming the little pine tree. I popped corn and managed to string enough of it to drape in festoons around the boughs, as the spicy aroma of apple pie filled the cabin.

Later, snug, warm and well-fed, but still feeling a little sorry for myself having to spend Christmas Eve alone, I was ready to settle in for my

"long winter's nap". Natasha watched as I added a large hardwood log to the fire and piled three old-fashioned quilts on the bed.

Snuggled under their protection, I drowsily wondered about the animals in the woods. *Are they safe and protected from the storm? Do they know about Christmas?*

Through the window I could see that the storm had nearly ended, leaving the trees in the pine forest near the cabin dressed in fluffy white robes. As the clouds parted, moonlight embellished the scene with a million sparkling diamonds.

I noticed two bright-red cardinals fluttering to a perfectly shaped pine just outside my window. The moonlight was so bright I could see they were carrying sprigs of holly and garlands of berries to the tree.

Woodland Dream

A large owl landed on a hardwood nearby, and its summoning call echoed through the silent forest. It wasn't long before other creatures came out from their snow-sheltered hiding places—a pair of graceful white-tailed deer...a fat brown beaver...a mother raccoon and two frisky babies.

Grayish brown rabbits appeared on the carpet of snow and hopped to join the group.

Next, a brown and white coyote joined the gathering, and then a small black bear took a position on the largest log near the tree. The creatures all stood, poised and ready.

Suddenly, a brilliant star appeared in the sky, positioned just above the tip of the tree. The starlight radiated in all directions, flooding the gathering of animals with a shimmering, golden glow!

For a moment, the animals basked in that light, sharing a silent celebration and forgetting struggle and survival. Then, a sudden noise jolted them, and just as quickly as they had come, they disappeared back into their woodland homes... *Ring-g-gg!*

I jumped, startled out of a deep sleep by the ringing of the telephone! It was Tom and the girls calling to wish me Merry Christmas. When I told them how I had decorated the cabin, they decided to pack our presents and drive up to join me once the roads were cleared!

I re-built the fire and made coffee, then sat by the window as the sun rose. Not a track or mark disturbed the pristine quilt of snow laid over the world. The beauty and silence charmed and beckoned.

I donned warm clothing, put on my snowshoes and headed out to feed the birds. When I opened the door, a whitetail deer and her twin fawns lifted their heads in curiosity before prancing off. Seeing them made me remember my dream about the cardinals' Christmas tree!

Could that special tree really exist? With Natasha bounding along beside me, I set out for the little pine forest in search of it. I found it easily, right where I knew it would be. There were no garlands or holly...but there *were* two cardinals perched near the top of the tree—a scarlet echo of my dream.

I hadn't been alone after all on Christmas Eve! Instead, I'd been part of a very special celebration. The cardinals had reminded me of what Christmas truly is: A time for every living creature to come together in peace and acceptance...a time to acknowledge and respect our differences ...while joining together to worship and celebrate.

I couldn't wait to share Christmas in the country with Tom and the girls when they arrived. I had the feeling it would be our best ever! ✺

Winter Woods

I walked through winter woods today,
And felt the brittle stillness there…
It held the somber trees in stay,
Mute, motionless, transfixed and bare,
Save for the ice that gave each one
A crystal glitter in the sun.

A universe without a sound!
A winter world of gray and white
In sylvan silence so profound
The sunbeams tip-toed in their flight.
The woods were host to me alone
And felt no heartbeat but my own.

—Herman T. Roberts, Hinsdale, Illinois

Spend more time in the country with our "family" of country-oriented magazines!

If you like this book, you'll love the four magazines published by the same firm—Reiman Publications. Each magazine brings you a bit of the country all year 'round.

Country is the magazine "for those who live in or long for the country." *Over 25%* of the people who have subscribed signed up for *2 years or more* after seeing just one sample copy!

They enjoy its *beautiful* photographs and fascinating features about people who love country life. They also like the fact it carries *no advertising*—just good reading.

Country offers something for every member of the family...a Country Decorating Section... Crafts and Food Sections...a Country Kids Section...essays and articles about country life...poetry..."tours" of country properties, inns and bed 'n' breakfasts...and color photos of country scenes so vibrant you'll want to cut them out and frame them!

Country Woman is the only magazine published *exclusively* for women who enjoy country living. Most of each issue is written *by readers*, as they exchange light-hearted ideas and anecdotes, country recipes, decorating ideas, crafts and nostalgic photos. And there's *no advertising*!

Each issue features a photo tour of one of the best kitchens in the country, plus elaborate food section which displays recipes in convenient "recipe card cutout" format. See why so many women call this their favorite magazine!

Country Handcrafts brings more than 20 fresh, original projects in each issue. There is *no advertising* in this magazine. Instead, it's filled cover-to-cover with

handcrafts. Each project is pictured in *full color* photos, and the FULL-SIZED pattern for every project is provided *right in the issue*, eliminating the need for time-consuming enlarging. Plus, you "meet" the designer of each craft through warm interviews.

Country Handcrafts is the magazine thousands of crafters look forward to for a variety of craft projects—cross-stitch, knit, crochet, wood-working and painting, basket-weaving, jewelry-making, applique, quilting and more!

Farm & Ranch Living isn't just for farmers! Anyone who likes the country will love "visiting" over 70 farms and ranches a year, without leaving the easy chair!

Each issue features four month-long, day-by-day diaries kept by farm and ranch families in different parts of the country, describing in detail their work, play and even their menus! There's a photo tour of a *beautiful* farm or ranch in each issue, including a "walk" through the house.

Readers reminisce about the "good old days" on the farm ...and tell about farmers' favorite cafes! Get a firsthand "feel" for farm and ranch life through the pages of *Farm & Ranch Living!*

TO ORDER a copy of this *A Year in the Country* book (at $17.98 plus $3.00 postage/handling), or to order any of the four magazines described here (sample copy $2.98 each; 1 year subscription $14.98 each) charge your order by calling toll-free **1-800/558-1013**.